# Pray continually,

1 Thessalonians 5:17

*Father, trouble is at my doorstep and I cannot seem to take control of it. God I need you to take control of my life, this day I give it all to you, my life is yours, my family is yours, my troubles I give it all to you. I submit my mind, will and emotions to you. Use me as you please, I give myself to you as a vessel you can use to do your will. Let your glory be revealed in my life and through my life. Transform me, reshape me, and mold me into my true identity which is in your image. Help me to understand my authority on earth, so that I can partner with Holy Spirit so that your will be done on earth as it is in heaven. Renew my mind, help me to focus on your kingdom that I am able to overcome this evil that has come against my family, in the name of your son Jesus Christ. AMEN*

# Day 1

*Call unto me and I will answer thee and show thee great and mighty things which thou knowest not*
*Jeremiah 33:3 (KJV)*

Finding out that your Wife/Husband had been unfaithful is devastating. The very person you have made a lifetime commitment to have gone astray. Trust have been broken, a friendship destroyed and a family shattered.

When this was my reality, I did not know what to do. How often do you hear people giving sound advice on how to get through such a devastating situation? The first response from society and sometimes from the church would be "DIVORCE".

***I called upon the Lord for help and he answered me!!!***
As a woman and a wife who made it through the attack and the sting of infidelity, I can tell you stay and FIGHT!

Fight for your Spouse!        _____
                                            (Spouse Name)

Fight for your Marriage!     _____
                                            (Marriage Date)

Fight for your Kid(s)           _____

_____        _____

_____        _____

# Day 2

*You will decide on a matter and it will be established for you and light will shine on your ways.*

## Job 22:28 (ESV)

When my husband's Infidelity was exposed. My entire life with him flashed before my eyes. Then the question came to me, "What will I do"?

I made the decision to fight not knowing what that really meant. The road ahead of that decision was not easy but it was worth it.

**Good things comes to those who wait, but great things are preserved for those who are willing to fight.**

**Pastor Shawn Echols**

With everything you have been faced with, you have to sit down and make a decision.

Are you willing to fight?

- I will not fight for my marriage. (Then no need to proceed in this journal)

- I will fight for my marriage. (Continue the journey set in this journal)

# Day 3

*Seek the Kingdom of God above all else, and live righteously, and he will give you everything you need.*
*Matthew 6:33 (NLT)*

Often times when I have heard this passage, it was in reference to finances. However, Holy Spirit revealed to me that during the season of warring for your family you need to seek HIM. In seeking God and His kingdom comes power and anointing. Yes I knew God, in fact I was a Youth Pastor & Dance Minister but this storm that has raged against me caused me to shift. I needed a fresh anointing to handle this battle.

What areas of your life that you can submit to God now that you have never done before?

# Day 4

*Let us review the situation together, and you can present your case to prove your innocence.*
*Isaiah 43:26 (NLT)*

**Many of the issues we face today are as a result of the actions of our forefathers. Someone in our bloodline have gave the enemy legal access to bring oppression in our lives. And that includes our finances, family and marriage. However, we can be free from it if we identify the issue and address it. Plea your case before God.**

Look back on your bloodline identify an issue or issues that has been plaguing your family from generation to generation. Check out your mother, grandmother, and great-grandmother. Or your father, grandfather and great grandfather.

# Day 5

## Prayer

Lord I give you thanks for your Son whom you have sent to die for our sins. Lord you gave us your only son that we may not perish but have everlasting life. Thank you for your word that is sharper than any two edged sword, your word that is spirit and gives life. Let your word be a lamp unto my feet and a light unto my path way. Thank you for providing for my every needs, thank you for the sun that rise each day and set each evening. Thank you Father for the air we breathe, Lord thank you for life!

Lord you are a great God, you are a holy God. You are the righteous Judge, the Lord God strong and mighty, and the Lord God mighty! Who can stand up against your glory? Every knee shall bow and every tongue shall confess that you are God. You are the God of the Living and not the dead. You reign forever. You are the Alpha and Omega, the beginning and the end. You are the first and the last. From Age to age you remain the same. You are the unchangeable God. You are faithful you are Holy. You are the Rock of Our salvation.

Lord I come before you in no other name but the name of your son Jesus the Christ. I repent for my sins, anything that I have done that is not pleasing to you in word, thought or deed.

Forgive me for I was foolish in my actions. I repent of the iniquity of my ancestors, every evil thing that they have done to bring reproach on our bloodline Lord I repent of it. I am guilty of all accusations that the enemy have brought against me but Father this day I ask for your forgiveness.

I come into agreement with the blood of Christ that testifies on my behalf and ask that you vindicate me of all accusations brought against me. Help me to fulfill everything that have written of me in the book of books. Save me from my accuser so that your glory may be revealed in my life and in the life of my family. Give me the scrolls concerning my life that I may eat of it, and do the things you have called me to do.

Every evil contract that have gone out against my life and the life of my family may it be canceled in the name of Jesus. Every wall that the enemy have erected it my life let it fall. Cut the umbilical cord that attaches me to the transgressions of my forefathers. Hide under the shadow of your wings. Lord give me your strength that I may endure through this battle, strengthen mine heart that I may not grow weary. Cause me to overthrow and overcome by the blood of the lamb.

Lord I thank you for hearing me case. Thank you for you are a just Judge, a righteous Judge. Lord thank you for ruling in my favor.

# Day 6

*Thus says the LORD: "In a time of favor I have answered you; in a day of salvation I have helped you; I will keep you and give you as a covenant to the people, to establish the land, to apportion the desolate heritages,*
*Isaiah 49:8 (ESV)*

I spent many days praying and crying to God. Every day seemed to be getting worse. My life felt as if it was reined. However, in spite of how things looked I held onto hope that God will come through for me. He did not come when I wanted Him but His timing was perfect.

Hold onto Hope. If you do not have something to give you hope you must find it and hold onto it. So whenever, you feel like giving up you have something to look back on.

What is giving you hope?

# Day 7

*This is what the Lord says. At just the right time, I will respond to you. On the day of salvation I will help you. I will protect you and give you as a covenant to the people, to establish the land, to apportion the desolate heritages.*

I spent many days praying and crying to God. Everyday seemed to be getting worse. My life felt as if it was ruined. However, in spite of how things looked I held onto hope that God will come through for me. He did not come when I wanted Him but He came just in time.

What have you spent many days crying to God about? Take this opportunity to pour your heart out once again, then speak of it NO more!

# Day 8

*Of David. Praise be to the LORD my Rock, who trains my hands for war, my fingers for battle. Psalms 144: 1 (NIV)*

When I made the decision to fight for my marriage, I really had no idea of what that meant. In fact, it seem as if I was losing the battle I was fighting. It was as if I was throwing my fist into the air. Coming out victorious was a blessing but I give full credit to Holy Spirit who was my guide.

Make a personal declaration, that although it may seem like you do not know how to fight God will show you!

_____

_____

_____

_____

_____

_____

_____

_____

_____

_____

# Day 9

*For we wrestle not against flesh and blood, but against principalities, against powers, against the rulers of the darkness of this world, against spiritual wickedness in high places.*
*Ephesians 6:12 (KJV)*

    I could not understand, how can a man treat a woman like a queen for years then turn around and treat her as if she is the dirt he walks on?  This is a question I am sure many women have, especially when there is no physical cause.  Well Ephesians 6:12 opened my eyes the moment I allowed Holy Spirit to show me what was going on in the life of my husband during such a difficult period of our lives.  The battle I was fighting was not against the physical man whom I was married to but it was against dark spiritual entities that was working in him

You may be a man and your wife's actions may have threw you into a ball of confusion.  How can my wife do this you might ask?

The moment you understand what you are fighting against, then you are ready for war!

# Day 10

*You can identify them by their fruit, that is, by the way they act. Can you pick grapes from thorn bushes, or figs from thistles?*
*Matthew 7:16 (NLT)*

If you are going to be successful in the fight for your marriage, you must know who you are fighting against. Many times we are praying against the wrong thing, then we get frustrated because we are not getting any results. The Lord showed me who the real enemy was and it was not my husband.  It was the spirit of lust and perversion, it was a generational curse upon my husband's bloodline, it was the spirit of adultery.

Before you go into warfare again, take a moment and identify who you are fighting against.  If you have no idea, I recommend you invest in a book called "Pigs in a Parlor" By Frank Hammond. It will open your eyes and bless your life.

# Day 11

*I have given you authority to trample on snakes and scorpions and to overcome all the power of the enemy. Nothing will harm you*
*Luke 10:19 (NIV)*

The authority over the enemy has already been given to you. There is nothing that can come up against your marriage that you do not have the authority to defeat. Fight for your family!

**My Declarations**: I am too young to divorce, I do not want to find another father for my kids, I do not want another husband. I will not let the enemy steal my family, I will fight for my marriage

**What is your declaration?**

# Day 12

*What therefore God has joined together let no man separate.*
*Mark 10:9 (NAS)*

Marriage between a man and a woman was set up and ordained by God. The enemy work overtime trying to disrupt this divine union. It is in your hand if you allow him to succeed. LET no man separate means you must do the work of defending your home. Not allowing the plans of the enemy to prevail! Yes I know it may seem out of reach because we have been programmed to believe we must ask God to do everything. Well now you understand the success of your marriage is in your hand.

Make a vow that you will not LET no one destroy your marriage.

# Day 13

*The wise woman builds her house, but with her own hands the foolish one tears hers down.*
*Proverbs 14:1 (NIV)*

You can build your house or tear it down. Be careful of your actions and your words. You may be going through a very difficult time right now. However, be alert and always think before you speak.

_____

_____

_____

_____

_____

_____

_____

_____

_____

_____

_____

_____

_____

_____

_____

_____

_____

# Day 14

*Those who control their tongue will have a long life; opening your mouth can ruin everything.*
*Proverbs 13:3 (NLT)*

The enemy will present to you many opportunities where you may have a right to speak harshly. However, that does not mean you must accept the opportunity. Many days you will need to chew your words like Wrigley's gum, but I will assure you it is not in vain.

Write down some scenarios where you were tempted to respond harshly but you didn't.

_____

_____

_____

_____

_____

_____

_____

_____

_____

_____

_____

_____

# Day 15

*Throw all your worry on him, because he cares for you.*
*1 Peter 5:7 (ISV)*

Fighting a battle is not easy.  However, do not burden yourself with worry.  Cast it all before the Lord He cares about you.

What are the things you need to cast before the Lord?

_____

_____

_____

_____

_____

_____

_____

_____

_____

_____

_____

_____

_____

_____

_____

_____

# Day 16

*Look to the LORD and his strength; seek his face always.*
*Psalm 105:4 (NIV)*

The thing you are going through is not in vain. However do not be consumed by it, do not turn away from God but turn to Him. Rise up, look to the Lord for His strength and continue to seek His face. You will win!

As you read this passage, what are you feeling in this moment?

_____

_____

_____

_____

_____

_____

_____

_____

_____

_____

_____

_____

# Day 17

*I consider that our present sufferings are not worth comparing with the glory that will be revealed in us.*
*Romans 8:18 (NIV)*

The rewards of the fight is greater than the pain from it. God is restoring marriages so that His glory may be revealed throughout the earth. You may believe that your present troubles are great, but let me tell you from experience it is not greater than the reward. I have been in the fight, I have endured the hurt, the shame, the feeling of rejection, the disrespect and much more. However, I fought and won now I am enjoying love that can only be experienced. Respect that sometimes I feel I don't deserve, support that I did not ask for. And the list goes on.

List some rewards that you would like to have and how God will get glory from them?

# Day 18

*Behold, the people shall rise up as a great lion, and lift up himself as a young lion: he shall not lie down until he eat of the prey, and drink the blood of the slain.*
*Numbers 23:24 KJV*

When a lioness goes after her prey, she is focused on what she wants and goes after it with all she's got. Go after your marriage with all you've got. Do not stop until the enemy becomes your prey and you have taken him down.

What do you think you need to do to rise as a lioness does?

_____
_____
_____
_____
_____
_____
_____
_____

# Day 19

*"Don't be afraid," the prophet answered. "Those who are with us are more than those who are with them.*
*2 Kings 6:16 (NIV)*

Many do not understand the fight for marriages. In many cases it seem like a lonely road, a journey you are traveling alone. More people are telling you to leave and divorce than are the ones saying stay and fight. The enemy seems to come at you with an army of minions, so much that it seems as if you are outnumbered. Let me encourage you, there are more for you than against you. As a wife or husband, the legal partner of your husband you have divine help. A legion of angels are on your side.

Write a prayer asking God to send out the Angels assigned to assisting you, ask Him to send your divine help.

# Day 20

*And they rose early in the morning, and went forth into the wilderness of Tekoa: and as they went forth, Jehoshaphat stood and said, Hear me, O Judah, and ye inhabitants of Jerusalem; Believe in the LORD your God, so shall ye be established; believe his prophets, so shall ye prosper.*
*2 Chronicles 20:20*

One day the Lord said to me "It's time to tell the story". My question was what story? From that moment on, the Lord began to playback my life when I was hit with infidelity in my marriage. He did this in order that not only I tell my story, but so that people will see what He is going to do. As a prophet of the Lord I can tell you, fight for your marriage because you will win!

Write your thoughts in this moment.

# *Day 21*

*And when you stand praying, if you hold anything against anyone, forgive them, so that your Father in heaven may forgive you your sins. "*
*Mark 11:25 (NIV)*

In order to heal from the hurt and pain you must forgive. Forgive the one who hurt you and the one that cause you pain. Forgiveness does not excuse them for what they have done, but it frees you from what has been done to you.

Who do you need to forgive and what do you need to forgive them for?

_____

_____

_____

_____

_____

_____

_____

_____

_____

_____

_____

_____

_____

_____

# Day 22

*Let us not become weary in doing good, for at the proper time we will reap a harvest if we do not give up.*
*Galatians 6:9 (NIV)*

A spiritual fight is just as hard as a physical fight or even harder. Either one can take a toll on you, it can get you drained to the point where you want to quit. In the fight for your marriage you cannot give up because you have a harvest to reap.

Ask God to give you His strength to keep going until you can reap your harvest.

_____

_____

_____

_____

_____

_____

_____

_____

_____

_____

_____

# Day 23

*And David was greatly distressed, for the people spoke of stoning him, because all the people were bitter in soul, each for his sons and daughters. But David strengthened himself in the LORD his God.*
*1 Samuel 30:6 (ESV)*

There are times when you will get discouraged, you have to rise up and be intentional about encouraging yourself during those times. Do not wait for someone to encourage you. In fact, you cannot wait for someone to encourage you.

Encouraging note to self.....

_____

_____

_____

_____

_____

_____

_____

_____

_____

_____

_____

# Day 24

*We also pray that you will be strengthened with all his glorious power so you will have all the endurance and patience you need. May you be filled with joy,*
*Colossians 1:11 (NLT)*

This is my prayer to you as you continue this journey! If you had to pray for someone who is experiencing the situation as you are, what would your prayer be for them?

_____

_____

_____

_____

_____

_____

_____

_____

_____

_____

_____

_____

_____

_____

# Day 25

*You will also decree a thing, and it will be established for you; and light will shine on your ways.*

It is important that day to day you are making positive decrees concerning your spouse, your marriage and your family!

When you make a decree you are setting laws in the atmosphere that must be established just because you spoke them.

Take some time, and write declarations from your heart concerning your spouse, your marriage and your family.

_____

_____

_____

_____

_____

_____

_____

_____

_____

_____

_____

_____

# Day 26

*For God hath not given us the spirit of fear; but of power,
and of love, and of a sound mind.
2 Timothy 1:7 (KJV)*

Fear is a tactic sent by the enemy to cause you to not move in your power and authority.  The moment you recognize it you must intentionally push even harder.  Faith and fear cannot dwell together.  Will you let faith or fear reside?

You can do it!

_____

_____

_____

_____

_____

_____

_____

_____

_____

_____

_____

_____

_____

_____

# Day 27

*Peace I leave with you; my peace I give to you. I do not give to you as the world gives. Do not let your hearts be troubled; do not be afraid.*
*John 14:27 (NIV)*

In this season there is something to be learned and there is something to gain.  Let the peace of the Lord be with and continue to push. If you do not give up you will reap.

_____

_____

_____

_____

_____

_____

_____

_____

# Day 28

*Death and life are in the power of the tongue: and they that love it shall eat the fruit thereof.*
*Proverbs 18:21 (KJV)*

By the power of your tongue you have the ability to speak life into your current situation. Use your tongue to bring life to your marriage. What you want to see speak it, where you want your spouse to be speak it. Speak it until you see it.

_____

_____

_____

_____

_____

_____

_____

_____

_____

_____

_____

_____

_____

_____

_____

_____

# Day 29

*Cast your cares on the LORD and he will sustain you;*
*he will never let the righteous be shaken.*
*Ps 55:22 (NIV)*

**The cares of this world are overwhelming, you do not
need to carry that with you. Give it over to God. Let go
and let God! You can trust Him because He will never
let the righteous be shaken. Are you righteous?**

What are some things you can think about that you need to
give over to God? Giving to God means you pray about it
and you enter into Gods rest. That thing you have prayed
about you do not get anxious over it.

_____

_____

_____

_____

_____

_____

_____

_____

_____

_____

_____

# Day 30

*If you believe, you will receive whatever you ask for in prayer*
*Matthew 21:22 (NIV)*

I have had the opportunity to counsel many during their time in the storm. My testimony of restoration have indeed blessed many. However, the problem is many do not believe that it can happen for them. Many are praying for restoration but do not believe that they will get what they are praying for. If you have stayed true to this journey I believe that you are strengthen in your spirit that you can now BELIEVE!

# Day 31

*Wait for the LORD; be strong, and let your heart take courage; wait for the LORD!*
*Psalms 27:14 (ESV)*

**That moment when you have done all you can, now it's time to Stand!**

While you are waiting, continue to journal your experiences, your thoughts and your feelings. No matter what happens in the wait, continue to trust the Lord and know that He is faithful and just to do what He promised.

_____

_____

_____

_____

_____

_____

_____

_____

_____

_____

_____

_____

_____

_____

_____

_____

_____

_____

_____

_____

2 Corinthians 10:5

Casting down imaginations, and every high thing that exalted itself against the knowledge of God, and bringing into captivity every thought to the obedience of Christ;

Jeremiah 23:29
"Is not My word like fire?" declares the LORD, "and like a hammer which
shatters a rock?

Ephesians 6:1

Therefore take up the full armor of God, so that when the day of evil comes, you
will be able to stand your ground, and having done everything, to stand.

Proverbs 13:3

The one who guards his mouth preserves his life; The one who opens wide his lips comes to ruin.

Proverbs 18:21

Death and life are in the power of the tongue, and those who love it will eat its
fruit.

Matthew 18:18

Truly I tell you, whatever you bind on earth will be bound in heaven, and whatever you loose on earth will be loosed in heaven.

1 Corinthians 15:57

But thanks be to God! He gives us the victory through our Lord Jesus Christ.

Ephesians 2:6
And hath raised us up together, and made us sit together in heavenly places in
Christ Jesus:

Ephesians 3:12

In whom we have boldness and access with confidence by the faith of him

Philippians 4:13
I can do all things through Christ who strengthened me.

Ephesians 3:16

I pray that out of the riches of His glory, He may strengthen you with power
through His Spirit in your inner being,

Colossians 1:11

"being strengthened with all power according to His glorious might so that you
may have full endurance and patience, and joyfully

2 Corinthians 12:9

But He said to me, "My grace is sufficient for you, for My power is perfected in weakness." Therefore I will boast all the more gladly in my weaknesses, so that the power of Christ may rest on me.

1 Corinthians 16:13

Be on the alert. Stand firm in the faith. Be men of courage. Be strong.

Exodus 15:11
Who among the gods is like you, LORD? Who is like you-- majestic in holiness,
awesome in glory, working wonders?

Ephesians 6:10

Finally, be strong in the Lord and in His mighty power.

1 Timothy 2:1

First of all, then, I urge that petitions, prayers, intercessions, and thanksgiving be offered on behalf of all men

Ephesians 6:18
Pray in the Spirit at all times, with every kind of prayer and petition. To this
end, stay alert with all perseverance in your prayers for all the saints.

2 Corinthians 12:

But He said to me, "My grace is sufficient for you, for My power is perfected in weakness." Therefore I will boast all the more gladly in my weaknesses, so that the power of Christ may rest on me.

Ephesians 3:12

In whom we have boldness and access with confidence

2 Samuel 22:35

"He trains my hands for battle, So that my arms can bend a bow of bronze.

Psalm 19:14
Let the words of my mouth and the meditation of my heart be acceptable in
Your sight, O LORD, my rock and my Redeemer.

Exodus 15:12

"You stretched out Your right hand, The earth swallowed them.

Deuteronomy 33:27
The eternal God is your refuge, and his everlasting arms are under you. He
drives out the enemy before you; he cries out, 'Destroy them!

Deuteronomy 7:2

and when the LORD your God delivers them before you and you defeat them,
then you shall utterly destroy them. You shall make no covenant with them and
show no favor to them.

Psalm 29:11

The LORD will give strength to His people; The LORD will bless His people
with peace

Deuteronomy 31:6

"Be strong and courageous, do not be afraid or tremble at them, for the LORD your God is the one who goes with you. He will not fail you or forsake you."

Deuteronomy 31:8
"The LORD is the one who goes ahead of you; He will be with you. He will not fail you or forsake you. Do not fear or be dismayed."

_____

_____

_____

_____

_____

_____

_____

_____

_____

_____

_____

_____

_____

_____

_____

_____

_____

_____

_____

Joshua 1:5
"No man will be able to stand before you all the days of your life. Just as I have
been with Moses, I will be with you; I will not fail you or forsake you.

1 Kings 8:57

"May the LORD our God be with us, as He was with our fathers; may He not leave us or forsake us,

Psalm 37:25

I have been young and now I am old, yet I have not seen the righteous forsaken
Or his descendants begging bread.

Philippians 4:6

Be careful for nothing; but in everything by prayer and supplication with
thanksgiving let your requests be made known unto God.

Proverbs 3:6

In all your ways acknowledge Him, And He will make your paths straight.

_____

_____

_____

_____

_____

_____

_____

_____

_____

_____

_____

_____

_____

_____

_____

_____

Romans 8:28

And we know that God causes everything to work together for the good of those
who love God and are called according to his purpose for them.

Proverbs 3:5

Trust in the LORD with all your heart and lean not on your own understanding;

Proverbs 28:26

He who trusts in his own heart is a fool, But he who walks wisely will be
delivered.

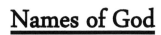

# Names of God

**Yahweh** = "I AM who I AM" or "I will be who I will be" (Exodus 3:13-14).

**Elohim** = "God" as in the Creator: In the beginning (Genesis 1:1).

**El Elyon** = "God" Most High" (Genesis 14:18-20).

**El Roi** = "God Who Sees" (Genesis 16:13-14).

**El Shaddai** = "God Almighty" or "God the All-Sufficient One" (Genesis 17:2-3).

**Adona**i = "Lord" (Exodus 4:10-12).

**Yahweh-Jireh** = "Yahweh will provide" or "I AM will provide" (Genesis 22:11-14).

**Yahweh-Rapha** = "Yahweh who heals": (Exodus 15:26).

**Yahweh—Nissi** = "Yahweh My Banner": (Exodus 17:16).

**Yahweh-Mekoddishkem** = "Yahweh Who Sanctifies You (Exodus 31:12).

**Yahweh-Shalom** = "Yahweh is Peace" (Judges 6:22-24).

**Yahweh-Sabaoth** = "Yahweh of Hosts" (Psalms 22:10).

**Yahweh-Raah** = "Yahweh My Shepherd" (Psalms 23:1).

**Yahweh-Tsidkenu** = "Yahweh Our Saving Justice (Jeremiah 23:5-6).

Ref: http://www.agapebiblestudy.com/documents/The%20Many%20Names%20of%20God.htm